MW01671141

Conquer With Your Seed

... and thy seed shall possess the gate of his enemies (Genesis 22:17b).

Joseph A. Alexander

NEW COVENANT PUBLICATIONS

Library of Congress Catalog Card Number: 97-69142
ISBN 1-57502-568-X

Unless otherwise indicated, Scriptures are taken from the King James Version of the Bible.

NEW COVENANT PUBLICATIONS
3601 Eastchester Road
Bronx, New York 10469

Printed in the USA by

MORRIS PUBLISHING

3212 East Highway 30 • Kearney, NE 68847 • 1-800-650-7888

Dedicated to my wife,
Mardette,
who, 18 years ago, covenanted with me to prepare lives for the kingdom of God.

Contents

Preface

In a wicked and perverted world, where hedonistic life-style is glamorized and the blatant rejection of God's righteousness has become the norm, is it possible to raise children who will arise to serve God and their country?

Is it possible to train our children as heirs of the same promise God has given to us the believing parents? Can they, under our mentorship as fathers and mothers, rise up to take the staff of God's righteousness and possess the gates of their enemies?

Well, I believe it is possible. It is possible for them to be heirs with us of the promises of God found in Scriptures. However, I am also convinced that it is going to take more than wishful thinking for this to happen.

It is, therefore, our hope that as you read this book, you will be challenged to sincerely and unreservedly invest in your child those values that God deems essential. The guarantee from the Lord is that you will never be ashamed.

Joseph A. Alexander

Scripture For Meditation

Genesis 17: 7. And I will establish my covenant between me and thee and thy seed after thee in their generations for an everlasting covenant, to be a God unto thee, and to thy seed after thee.

Isaiah 44: 3 For I will pour water upon him that is thirsty, and floods upon the dry ground: I will pour my spirit upon thy seed, and my blessing upon thine offspring:

Acts 2: 39 For the promise is unto you, and to your children, and to all that are afar off, even as many as the Lord our God shall call.

Jeremiah 32: 39 And I will give them one heart, and one way, that they may fear me for ever, for the good of them, and of their children after them.

Chapter 1

God's Promise

The creation of man proceeded with God's resolve. He determined what man's role will be on earth..This crown of all creation is God's rightful representative. It was God who through His infinite wisdom set the stage for man to have dominion over the earth along with his seed. The word of God clearly states:

And God blessed them, and God said unto them, be fruitful, and multiply, and replenish the earth, and subdue it, and have dominion over the fish of the sea, and over the fowl of the air, and over every living thing that moveth upon the earth."

(Genesis 1:28)

Here, a promise was given by God Himself to Adam and Eve - to conquer and dominate. They were to dominate the world around them - the sea, the air and the earth. Nothing was left out. It was never the plan of God for man to be dominated by the devil.

When God made the promise to Adam and Eve, it incorporated their offspring. In other words, in making this promise to them, God was also addressing their unborn children. That is the principle that God operates by. When God told Noah that He would destroy the earth, did He forget Noah's children? No.

"But with thee will I establish my covenant; and thou shalt come into the ark, thou, and thy sons ..."

(Genesis 6:18).

God's plan was that both Noah and his children would be saved. When God also called Abraham, He included his children in the covenant:

> *"And I will establish my covenant between me and thee and thy seed after thee in their generations for an everlasting covenant, to be a God unto thee, and to thy seed after thee."*
>
> *(Genesis 17:7).*

A covenant consists of two parties. In this case, the Almighty God was on one side; on the other was Abraham and his seed. God

The children belong to God and we are their custodians to bring them up in the way of the Lord

did not expect the parent to serve Him at the exclusion of their children. As a matter of fact, God would often hold parents responsible for the failure of their children to serve Him.

The children of Godly parents, as being heirs together with their parents, is also taught in the New Testament. On the day of Pentecost, Peter, under the inspiration of the Holy Spirit, pointed out the inclusion of the children in the blessing of the Gospel. He said,

> *"For the promise is unto you, and to your children..."*
>
> *(Acts 2:39)*

And again, in another address, Peter pointed out:

> *"Ye are the children of the prophets, and of the covenant which God made with our fathers, saying unto Abraham, And in thy seed shall all the kindred of the earth be blessed."*
>
> *(Acts 3:25)*

Even when the gentile jailor asked to be saved in Philippi, Paul did not address the salvation of the jailor alone for he knew the mind of God, that when the father gets saved, the children should get saved too. If the parents are walking with God, the children should also walk with God. Such has been the view of God, and this remains the same. To the question of the jailor, Paul declared,

> *"Believe on the Lord Jesus, and thou shalt be saved, and thy house."*
>
> *(Acts 16:31)*

When God issues a promise to the parents, the children are part of it because they

> ***Do not, for a moment, wonder if it is God's perfect will for your children to be part of the covenant of salvation.***

are part and parcel of us. What affects one affects the other. God knows this and He has made provision for us in His Word. Do not, for a moment, wonder if it is God's perfect will for your children to be part of the covenant of salvation. Nothing can be clearer from Scriptures than that. It is, however, very important that you prepare them to inherit God's promise with you. This is your duty.

The children belong to God and we, as their parents, are their custodians to bring them up in the way of the Lord. When Moses went to Pharaoh to seek permission to worship God on the mount for three days, Pharaoh suggested that they should go without their children. This notion, Moses blatantly refused. He could not conceive the idea of worshipping God without their children. What message would he be sending them? One that allowed children to worship the gods of the heathen as long as their parents worshipped the true God?

How could they go on a spiritual journey and enjoy the blessings of God while their children remained in spiritual ignorance or apathy? To such absurd suggestion, Moses answered Pharaoh:

> *"... We will go with our young and with our old, with our sons and with our daughters, with our flocks and with our herds will we go; for we must hold a feast unto the LORD"*
>
> *(Exodus 10:9).*

Such must be our attitude. We will not lose our children to the world. They will not serve the god of this world. They will not end up at the wrong side of the law. Instead, they will love the God we love. They will serve Him. We will not lose them to the moral decline of this generation. They are our responsibility and we will not fail in our duty in this regard. One day, we will be brought to give account to God how we raised them up.

Worldly Influence

We live in a very difficult generation where the influence of parents and the church on their children is being superimposed by the false glamor of Hollywood. Hollywood is now setting the moral standards for our children who innocently are adapting their life-styles to such depravity. But the children are not being presented with the whole picture, that behind the mask of glamor and fame is a void that is not being filled, no matter how they try to cover it up. They lure our children to the world view that they are their own bosses, that they can choose whatever they want to do, be it drugs, or crime, premarital or extramarital sex.

The secular media is also following suit. The impact of the media upon the social development of our children is so derogatory that it will take a spiritual revolution to gain them back. Immediate revolution is what it will take to turn the wheel in the right direction.

Immediate revolution is what it will take to turn the wheel in the right direction

The problem is further compounded by the apparent apathy of some parents. They refuse to see the warning signs which will destroy their children and surely translate into heart ache in the future. They seem so indifferent to the impact the world is making on their children. They are being blindfolded into believing that we are living in a different generation and allowances contrary to the Word of God should be made for fear that they might lose them.

The only wise option, they see, is to compromise with them. As long as they agree to go to church, they are free to watch any program on TV, play any music that they like and keep the company of friends they choose. And of course, they may have objectionable pictures of Hollywood stars in their rooms. At least, that way, they stay at home.

There can be no compromise of our children with the world

But, the sad reality is that ,it is the fastest way to lose them. There can be no compromise of our children with the world. The Bible makes no compromise on relationships with the world. The command is to be separate, not in interaction but in principles of living. Christian parents who have compromised and allowed their children to live by the standards of the world did not expect what they saw at the end of the tunnel. They gave their children leeway. What has been the outcome? Utter disregard for what the church and the Bible stand for.

Various Perversions

Sexual perversion has reached a height that those who lived three generations ago would have shuddered in disbelief. No longer are teen children ashamed to talk about sex in any shape or fashion. They are proud to declare that they sleep with their boyfriends on an on-going basis. As a matter of fact, they pat themselves on the shoulders that they do not have more than one sexual partner at a time.

Thank God, some of them are realizing the fact that they cannot play with fire and not be burned. Even the secular TV in a few cases, now advocates abstinence as the best and safest deterrence to teen age pregnancy and AIDS. It is a departure from the long-held view. A surgeon general under Clinton Administration advocated for free sex and even provision of condom for the teens. No wonder, her view degenerated to a point that President Clinton Administration let her go for fear of smearing the Democratic Party in the public eye.

Sexual perversion has reached a height that those who lived three generations ago would have shuddered in disbelief

We are indeed living in an age where we do not know what to expect next. Homosexuality is rapidly becoming the norm. And our teenagers are not immuned to it. Teenagers are going in droves to new life-styles. They want to explore a new thing, and the government, to some extent, is encouraging it.

Our public educational system had no choice but to distribute condoms to its students. The textbooks had to be changed to accommodate teachers with the new found life-style.

Violence continues to increase among our

youth. Gone are the days, when the grave sins of school-age children were limited to lateness, rudeness to teachers, chewing gum, talking at wrong times. Now, we deal with drugs in our schools. We deal with guns within the four walls of our classrooms. It is being advocated now that the public schools should

It is time to rise and worship God with our children

wear uniform. One of the reasons advanced was **the safety of public school children.** Safety from what? And from who? From **gangsters who might have mistaken their identity and hurt them.**

Few years ago, we set aside huge amounts of money to build schools, maintain them and to pay teachers. But those days are now gone. Now we need extra money for security guards, and the police to guard our schools, and metal detectors to keep guns and other dangerous weapons out. *This is the age in which our children are being raised.*

A Call To Action

Can we remain apathetic and hope that they will be all right without a positive and definite move for a change? Can we be so naive as to think that our children will not be affected by their peers who hold different views from what is being taught to our children at school and at home? Do we dare neglect the thought that the enemy of our soul is not in the least interested in the souls of our children? If there was ever a time for a call to dramatic action, it is now. The need is everywhere. The time is now. It is time to rise and serve God with our children

Josh McDowel in a Why-Wait campaign research brought out this unimaginable statistics: by the time a child reaches the age of 12, he/she has watched about 9,962 hours of sexual or violent crime in the United States on TV.

Should it surprise any of us that by that age, she/he has lost virginity - a gift that they are supposed to reserve for their spouse? Is it any surprise that teenage pregnancy is on the increase, where children are having children? They have lost their childhood to the worldly system. An advertisement on the TV about a 15 year old who is now a mother and laments that she has lost her childhood, gives a vivid picture to what our children are being exposed to.

Yes, this is the age during which our children are being raised up in. Can we ignore these facts, and pretend that they are not there? Or can we be so naive as to think that it will never happen to our children, even though we allow them to watch the same programs that

The spiritual teachings of the church have been replaced by secular humanism, hedonism...

these other children are watching and attend the same schools! Can we be so impractical to imagine that it will not affect our children when our children rub shoulder with these children whose parents know no better! Dare we just shrug it off as a passing fling in youth, and hope that one day, a positive change will catapult all the children to the righteous side of morals. Such positivism, as good as it seems, is naive, at the very best.

From experience in my travels, the moral decline in Europe is even worse. Africa and South America where moral values are appreciated are also witnessing moral decline, and they are not too far behind in the moral decline of the United States. The world seems to be in a moral chaos where even the secular governments are powerless about what to do. Do we as a people of promise have an answer?

In the United States, the Ten Commandments have been ruled out. Prayer has become a taboo. The spiritual teachings of the church have been replaced by secular humanism, hedonism (if-it-feels-good-do-it philosophy) of the times and by the imagination of the teachers who have little spiritual convictions of the church. Is it any wonder that the children are turning out the way they are! Is it not a matter of sowing and reaping what we have sown in our children!

Spiritual Influence

This is not just a moral battle. It goes far beyond the moral struggle. The struggle is first and foremost spiritual. We are living in the last days where the judgement of Satan is about to begin. And he is definitely not holding his hands in idleness awaiting the inevitable judgment. It is also a great conquering time in human history.

Satan knows that if he could conquer the children, he has conquered the world. The children are our future. This fact is being capitalized by the enemy of our soul. Unless the people of God understand the person behind the moral decline of the children, then, all efforts of reformation or rehabilitation will prove futile. It is not the government of the United States or the United Nations for that matter that will bring the necessary change. They

The battle is spiritual in nature, and must be fought with spiritual ammunitions

themselves are confused and live in spiritual darkness because the god of this world, Satan, has blinded their eyes.

The battle is spiritual in nature, and must be fought with spiritual ammunitions. As Christian parents, we must fight for our children. We must give them a good start in life.

God, who knows the beginning to the end, has made provision by which we will not fall prey to the dictates of the world around us

We must expose them to the things of the Lord in the prime of their lives, and rest assured that God in heaven will see them through. We will do our part and leave the rest to God.

The Bible is not silent on how to raise our children nor how to wage the war. God, who knows the beginning to the end, has made provision by which we will not fall prey to the dictates of the world around us. Let us turn to the Bible and see how men of old raised their children.

Scripture For Meditation

Genesis 6: 9 These are the generations of Noah: Noah was a just man and perfect in his generations, and Noah walked with God.

Genesis 6: 18 But with thee will I establish my covenant; and thou shalt come into the ark, thou, and thy sons, and thy wife, and thy sons' wives with thee.

Genesis 7: 1. And the LORD said unto Noah, Come thou and all thy house into the ark; for thee have I seen righteous before me in this generation.

Hebrews 11: 7 By faith Noah, being warned of God of things not seen as yet, moved with fear, prepared an ark to the saving of his house; by the which he condemned the world, and became heir of the righteousness which is by faith.

Chapter 2

Noah And His Children

Genesis chapter six gives a vivid description of the moral state of the world in the time of Noah.

> *"And God saw that the wickedness of man was great in the earth, and that all the imagination of the thought of his heart was only evil continually."*
>
> *(Genesis 6:5)*

God saw the moral decline of this generation and He described them as wicked. As a matter of fact, the wickedness was great in the sight of God. In the sight of the people they might have considered themselves as being free to do whatever they wanted to do. After all, there was the freedom of speech and expression! The right to do what they enjoyed doing. They did not see the wickedness of their actions, and they did not feel accountable to God for their life-style. If it felt good, they did it.

But the source of their actions was embedded in the heart. Their heart was not right. And the Bible says that it grieved God that He ever made them. They forgot the fact that they did not make themselves. They had a creator to whom they must give account. They were not their own. But God's patience lasts for so long. A day of reckoning will come one day. It is a matter of time.

But in the midst of this decline in morals and spirituality of the race was a man. His name was Noah. The Bible describes Noah as a good man in the midst of the corruption of his generation.

"Noah was a just man and perfect in his generation and Noah walked with God. And Noah begat three sons, Shem, Ham and Japheth."

(Genesis 6:9,10)

In the spiritual decline of his generation, Noah walked with God. He was married like everyone else. He had a family - a wife and three sons. The sons were also married. They were not living in monasteries or in jungles away from the wicked society. They lived among the wicked.

In the spiritual decline of his generation, Noah walked with God

"The earth also was corrupt before God, and the earth was filled with violence. And God looked upon the earth and, behold, it was corrupt; for all flesh had corrupted his way upon the earth."

(Genesis 6:11,12.

Such was the description of the society in which Noah lived and brought up his children. The question is: how could Noah raise his children without loosing them to the world?

I am convinced that the answer to this question lies in Noah's relationship with God. Genesis 6:9 states specifically that Noah walked with God. But he did not walk alone with God. He included his children in this spiritual journey. Notice that Noah had a measure of revelation from God. It was not half as expanded as we have today. But with the little he had, he passed it on to his children.

With deliberation on his part, he systematically taught his children the whole counsel of God. He taught them that God has a kingdom to which he wanted them to belong. He did not leave his children to be instructed by this corrupt system. He was bent on overcoming evil with good. He knew it could be done. And he did it.

He had a choice of walking alone with God and pay little regard to the spiritual condition of his children. Mind you, children are children in every generation. And believe it or not, children often influence children. But the children of Noah's generation did not have a negative influence on the children of Noah. How could that be? I believe total separation is necessary at times. There could be no compromise. To compromise is to leave room for the devil.

Noah's Determination

Noah had purposed within himself that he would not leave his children behind. He did not lose hope nor doubt that his children would make it in their wicked generation. He knew that they could make it. This was in an age, where the Bible had not been written. They did not have much revelation of God. Historical dealings of God on behalf of Israel had not been written. The examples of men and

You cannot destroy a system to which you have sold yourself and your family

women who walked with God were few and far between. Yet, here was this man, alone in this world of sin and corruption, determined to serve God with his family.

When the divine judgment was about to be meted out, Noah could be saved. He was not part of the worldly system. He had not sold his children to its dictates and thinking. You cannot destroy a system to which you have sold yourself and your family. Why? Because to do so is to destroy yourself.

Noah raised his children in a sin-ridden society

Put differently, you cannot condemn a system of which you are an integral part because the human disposition is to self protect.

If you yourself have been going partially with the world system you will find yourself in a tough spot. If you have permitted your children to follow the dictates of the media and Hollywood, or what their school mates are doing or what their reprobate teacher or school system is teaching, it becomes difficult to combat.

The combat must begin within. You need to examine yourself and repent of any compromise you might have made with the world. You must break the unequal yoke that has tied you to the world.

> *"Be ye not unequally yoked together with unbelievers: for what fellowship hath righteousness with unrighteousness? and what communion hath light with darkness? Wherefore come out from among them, and be ye separate, saith the Lord, and touch not the unclean thing; and I will receive you And will be a Father unto you, and ye shall be my sons and daughters, saith the Lord Almighty"*
>
> *(2 Corinthians 6:14, 17,18).*

This is the promise of God - that immediately you break the tie with the world, then the Lord will receive you. You may already be born again, spirit filled, but still have this tie with the world. There is restoration in God.

After you have broken the tie, then can you help your child to also break the tie with the world and its thought system.

Noah raised his children in a sin-ridden society. It was not a half-haphazard training. It was focussed. It was a conscious effort on his part to see that his children were brought up in the way of the Lord.

It may be argued that the Bible does not say directly that Noah's children were godly. But every suggestion shows otherwise. When

> ***Noah's children... had been trained in the ways of the Lord... They were used to obeying their parents***

God was going to destroy the world, he included Noah's children. If the children had been ungodly, they would not have gone with their father and mother. They would have laughed at them like the rest of the world. They would not have believed in the possibility of the rain destroying the earth. They would not have identified with the prophecy of God to their father

But we read nothing of such rebellion. They must have helped their father to build the ark at the ridicule of their peers. Who says that there was no peer pressure in the days of Noah? It is there in every generation.

Noah's children, however, had been trained in the ways of the Lord. So when obe-

Rest assured, therefore, that God wants you to be saved - you and your household.

dience became critical, they did not disappoint their father for they were used to obeying their parents. They were brought up to know that their father was in touch with God and knew the voice of God. It was not a time for them to begin to argue with their father. They were taught otherwise. The Bible says to train up a child in the way he should go, and when he is grown he would not depart from it.

One of the gifts you can give to your children is respect and obedience to you, so that during the critical times, they will listen to you.

The knowledge of the Scriptures is the foundation of academic knowledge

God saw the faithfulness of Noah in raising his children to follow the Lord. What does He see in you? How do you think God will rate you in this aspect?

Noah's concern and attention to the spiritual condition of his children paid off. They were not destroyed with the world system. They were spared from the flood that God was about to bring. Noah was not saved without his household. He had done his part. It was now time to reap.

Do not be afraid to bring up your children in the ways of the Lord. It is for their own good. It is good medicine to them. A child needs guidance. A large percentage of people in prison say that they did not receive adequate correction from their parents. Maybe the parents had no time for them. Perhaps, they were afraid that they might leave home in the future. Whatever the reason might be, the children grew up without firmness and correction. And they landed in prisons because they were not demanded to obey.

Noah should be a challenge to many parents today who feel overwhelmed by the moral corruption in which their children are growing. His life offers hope to the hopelessness of the present situation. He made it. He brought up his children and so can you. You can resolve within you that your children too, will be raised up to fear God. They will be raised to respect their parents and authority. If you trust God to give you wisdom and withal to give them this heritage that cannot be taken away from them, you will not be disappointed. Praise the Lord.

God's Covenant With You

God wants to establish His covenant with you and your children. He does not want to focus on you alone and forget your children. This fact needs to be accepted. Do not view God as not being interested in your children. He is. And He has made adequate plans for them. God expects you to pass it on to your children. Rest assured therefore that God wants you to be saved - you and your household. The wickedness of Noah's generation had reached its zenith.

> *"And God said unto Noah, The end of all flesh is come before me; for the earth is filled with violence through them; and, behold, I will destroy them with the earth."*
>
> *(Genesis 6:13).*

Then came the word of promise to Noah,

> *"But the Lord said to Noah, Come thou and all thy house into the ark; for thee have I seen righteous before me in this generation"*
>
> *(Genesis 7:1).*

And the result? Noah and his children were saved from the flood.

It is my conviction that Christian education is paramount to the raising of a child. The public schools have excluded the Bible out of their system. Why send children to school? Is it not to learn? But what are they learning in these public schools? What values are being ingrained in them? What effect is this education having on our children?

A child of six is ready to enter the public

They need to be around godly teachers who are committed both to academic excellence and spiritual strength

school. He or she is very vulnerable at this age. He is easily swayed in his own thinking. He spends an average of six hours in school, in a system that does not acknowledge God. In fact, in some cases, the child is told that God is not important in his life.

I am of the conviction that parents should send their children to a Christian school where Christian values are being inculcated into the moral fibre of their precious children. They need to be around godly teachers who are committed both to academic excellence and spiritual strength. They need to know that education is not complete without God. The knowledge of the Scriptures is the foundation of academic knowledge. This must be ingrained in their minds from a tender age.

Scripture For Meditation

Genesis 12: 7 And the LORD appeared unto Abram, and said, Unto thy seed will I give this land: and there builded he an altar unto the LORD, who appeared unto him.

Genesis 18: 17, 19 And the LORD said, Shall I hide from Abraham that thing which I do. ... For I know him, that he will command his children and his household after him, and they shall keep the way of the LORD, to do justice and judgment; that the LORD may bring upon Abraham that which he hath spoken of him.

Hebrews 11:8,9 By faith Abraham, when he was called to go out into a place which he should after receive for an inheritance, obeyed; and he went out, not knowing whither he went. By faith he sojourned in the land of promise, as in a strange country, dwelling in tabernacles with Isaac and Jacob, the heirs with him of the same promise

Chapter 3

Abraham and His Children

Let us face it. The days might be dangerous but God promised to be with us. In the heathen country of Canaan, Abraham raised Isaac. He trained him in the midst of wickedness of the Canaanites, the Jebusites and all the forces that you can imagine. Like Noah's children, Isaac was not contaminated by the mentality of his generation. But there was a father and a mother who were committed to the purpose of God which included the training up of the precious seed of promise whose name was Isaac. They were training him to rise up and serve so that God might fulfill the promise made to him.

In an unprecedented move, when God wanted to test the obedience of Abraham, His friend, the involvement of his son became paramount. Isaac, having been raised by his father in a godly way, responded to the will of his father to honor God.

The proof of Abraham's love and faithfulness to God rested in part, on how he brought up the seed of promise - Isaac.

The proof of Abraham's love and faithfulness to God rested in part, on how he brought up the seed of promise - Isaac. Let us consider the dynamics of raising up children as provided in the Scriptures.

The Test

God wanted to prove Abraham his friend whom He promised to give Canaan for eternal possession, and indeed the rest of the world. In regards to this promise the Bible records:

> *"After these events, God tested and proved Abraham and said to him: take now thy son, your only son Isaac, whom you love and go to the region of Moriah; and offer him there as a burnt offering upon the mountain of which I will tell you."*
>
> *(Gen. 22:1,2 ampl)*

Like an obedient servant, Abraham responded to God's bid. Notice that the demand was not made on Abraham's head, but on that of his son, a tougher demand. The proof of how he raised up Isaac was being tested to the core. Abraham went with his son to Mount Moriah.

The Bible tells us that as they approached the mount of sacrifice, the curious Isaac asked the father, "my father, here is the wood and the fire, but where is the lamb for the sacrifice?" Can you imagine what must have been going through Abraham's mind? He was on his way to a mount where he was to offer this son of promise.

Can you imagine the conflict between his spirit and his reasoning faculty? On the one hand, he knew this child would survive him for he was the promised heir. On the rational side, how could a sacrifice and a dead son inherit the promise of God? To the curious question of his son, Abraham affirmed to him that God would provide a lamb for Himself.

The next scene we encounter is the dramatic obedience of Abraham as he raised up his hand to kill his son. The scene ends with another dramatic move of God. The Bible records:

"But the Angel of the Lord called to him from heaven and said, Abraham, Abraham,! He answered, Here I am. And he said to him,

do not lay your hand on the lad or do anything to him for now I know that you fear and revere God, since you have not held back from Me or begrudged giving me your son, your only son"

(Gen. 22:11,12 amp).

We must not overlook an important fact. Why did Isaac not resist his father's move to sacrifice him at the altar of God? He could have, if he had wanted to. But I believe that it had been ingrained in him that God's orders must be carried out without question. That was how he had been brought up. It was a matter of fact to him, even at such tender age, when most of his peers would have been rebellious in this period (teenage years).

But not Isaac. He had been raised well. He had been taught about the fear of God. He

How are you training your child to respond to the love, power and righteousness of God?

had been taught by his able father that God is a good God who never fails. No wrongdoing could proceed from Him. He had promised him that he, Isaac, would be the sole heir of the father. He was the long-awaited son of promise from a God who never fails. Even if God were to ask him to be sacrificed, He had power to raise him back to life. One fact stood out - God's faithfulness and goodness.

What an excellent training! A training that would allow a teenager to allow his father to abuse and even kill him - to please God. How are you training your child to respond to the love, power and righteousness of God?

What sacrifice and time would have gone into the training that Abraham and Sarah gave to their son to reach such excellence in obedience!

In the Christian school education, we insist on a God-centered education where the Bible is the greatest source of moral and spiritual education with the utmost drive for academic excellence. This balance is needed in a world where both moral and even academic excellence is being eroded.

This balanced education, unfortunately, is not cheap today. It is even worse, because Christian parents send their children to anti-God schools in the name of free education.

When the home spiritual education is coupled with the godly education they are receiving from school, it will surely make a definite indelible mark on the heart of your child.

Abraham considered the way of God and the promise of God as more valuable than the cheap and free education of the land of Canaan.

The Everlasting Blessing

Abraham and Isaac are now reunited because God provided the actual lamb for sacrifice.

> *"The Angel of the Lord called to Abraham from heaven a second time and said, I have sworn by Myself says the Lord that since you have not withheld from Me your only son. In blessing I will bless you and in multiplying I will multiply your seed like the stars of the heavens and like the sand on the seashore. And your seed will possess the gate of his enemies. And in your seed shall all the nations of the earth be blessed."*
>
> *(Gen. 22:15-18 amp. emphasis, mine)*

Both the father and the son participated in obeying God. But the responsibility lies squarely on the parents to teach their children to obey God. It is the father and the mother who must set the standard, and set the parameters of operation in the family, more so in a wicked world such as ours. We are aliens in this world. We are different and must act so. We live in the world but we are not part of it.

This fact needs to be ingrained in our children. Their moral standards must not be based on the standard the world has set. Their standard must be measured by the standard the Bible provides.

Let me, once again, ask the question: What kind of investment are you putting in your child? The kind of foundation you are laying in your child's life does count. You must be the model of obedience to God in every situation which your child can see. Actions often speak louder than words. Your faithfulness in simple things such as attending midweek Bible study, giving to missions work and to the poor, could go a long way, even though you are struggling fi-

> *From their cradle, children should be taught to reverence the Word of God.*

nancially. Let them see the sacrifice you are making to live up to the standard of God's Word.

When the home spiritual education is coupled with the Godly education they are receiving from school, it will surely make a definite indelible mark on the hearts of your children.

Scripture For Meditation

Deuteronomy 11: 19 And ye shall teach them your children, speaking of them when thou sittest in thine house, and when thou walkest by the way, when thou liest down, and when thou risest up.

Deuteronomy 4: 9 Only take heed to thyself, and keep thy soul diligently, lest thou forget the things which thine eyes have seen, and lest they depart from thy heart all the days of thy life: but teach them thy sons, and thy sons' sons.

Ephesians 6: 4 And, ye fathers, provoke not your children to wrath: but bring them up in the nurture and admonition of the Lord.

Psalms 78: 3 Which we have heard and known, and our fathers have told us.

Chapter 4

The Mandate

Hear, O Israel, the LORD our God is one LORD, and thou shalt love the LORD thy God with all thine heart, and with all thy soul, and with all thy might. And these words which I command thee this day shall be in thine heart. And thou shalt TEACH them diligently unto thy children, and shall talk of them when thou sittest in thine house and when thou walkest by the way and when thou liest down and when thou risest up."

(Deuteronomy 6:4-7)

Parents: Primary Educators

The parents are the primary educators of their children in spiritual matters. From their cradle, children should be taught to reverence the Word of God. Among the Hebrew chil-

Your purpose is two fold: instruct them in the way that they should go, and more importantly, impart to them love for God and His Word.

dren, they value the religious education of their children so much so that they are not exposed to any other learning, talk less of another religion, until the age of ten.

Teaching

Look closely at the commandment of God to parents: parents are to teach their children. Two words are important here. Teaching in-

One thing God insists on is that Israel should teach their children about His dealings and deliverances,

volves a systematic impartation of knowledge. In other words, they are to be instructed in the things of God. They must teach them the precepts of God. They must teach them the acts of God. One thing God insists on is that Israel should teach their children about His dealings and deliverances, like the exodus out of Egypt, the parting of the Red Sea and so on. It is the responsibility of parents to pass on to their children the true account of God's miracles.

Children love to hear stories. And the Bible is full of true accounts of miracles.

Teach your children about the Flood, tell them about the miracles of Christ. Tell them about the miracles in the Acts of the apostles. Let them be aware of God's dealings with His people in the past.

Also impart to them the basic teachings of the Bible. Teach them about what God frowns at and what He smiles upon. Teach them about the Ten Commandments. Establish them in the knowledge of the Bible. Instil in them the love for God's Word. Teach directly from the Bible, and you may buy good Bible stories which you may read at Bed time for them. Let them commit Scriptures to memory. Their brain is young and "absorbent." And they will love it, beside the fact that it is good for their overall educational discipline. A four year old can memorize 1 Corinthians 13:8 which says, *"love never fails."* Brief but memorized.

Do not overtask them. Your purpose is two fold: instruct them in the way that they should go, and more importantly, impart to them love for God and His Word. Hence, wisdom is essential to do this.

Diligence And Consistency

The other important word in this verse is diligence. Yes, it is not a haphazard thing. It is not a matter of whether you feel like or not. There must be a level of diligence here. You are dealing with, not only the future of your children, but their eternal destiny. You do not want to raise children who will rise up and go against the Word of God because of lack of diligence.

What does diligence include? Talk it to them as often as possible, and be consistent.

Three places the Bible says you should teach your children are: in your house, outside the house, in the morning and at night. Here,

While you are at work, your child should be where the Word of God is honored and taught.

the Lord covered time and space. If you are not in your house, you are outside of it. What God is telling you as parent in essence, is that you teach your children anywhere and everywhere. While you are at work, your child should be where the Word of God is honored and taught.

The Bible says it is to be in the morning and in the evening. That means every time.

Jesus says that you will know the truth and the truth will set you free.

Does it mean you should shuffle the Bible down their throat without breathing space? NO. But you need to use wisdom. Sin is being shuffled down their throat every day. But let the Word of God be the companion of your child.

Decorate their rooms with nice Christian posters. When they become teen agers they will not want a nude picture in their room. You see, their taste bud is set.

Just as God instructed Israel to hold on to the Word of God in the land that they will possess so Christian parents are to arm their children with God's Word in order to possess the riches of the heathen.

If Israel were to possess the land then obedience to God's commandment was a must. In other words, strength to possess the land could be achieved through obedience. But God was not thinking only of the short term. He had future generations in mind. Each generation must pass on the baton to the next. Each generation must be faithful. There can be no broken link.

Scripture For Meditation

2Corinthians 10: 3 For though we walk in the flesh, we do not war after the flesh. 4 (For the weapons of our warfare are not carnal, but mighty through God to the pulling down of strong holds;)

1Timothy 1: 18. This charge I commit unto thee, son Timothy, according to the prophecies which went before on thee, that thou by them mightest war a good warfare.

Zechariah 4: 6 Then he answered and spake unto me, saying, This is the word of the LORD unto Zerubbabel, saying, Not by might, nor by power, but by my spirit, saith the LORD of hosts.

1Corinthians 1: 18 For the preaching of the cross is to them that perish foolishness; but unto us which are saved it is the power of God.

Chapter 5

The Challenge

Before we drop the pen, let me encourage you as mothers and fathers who have faithfully sown the seed to the best of your knowledge. Perhaps you have done all you could to instill the Word of God in your child in his early years. You took him to church faithfully. You taught him the fear of God. You encouraged him to love God, His Word and His people. Yet, he has not turned out to be who you want him to be. The seed of God's Word does not appear to have germinated in his life. Instead of a godly adult, you are faced with

With this confidence, you can plead your case before the Almighty God.

one that has no interest in the things of God.

He has left the faith of his parents for worldly pleasures. He leads a life-style that you are not proud of. Drugs, booze, thefts, adultery, fornication have claimed him. He is in a circle of friends who have no respect for God's Word. He may not even be involved in blatant immorality, but he is cold in the things of God. He hates to come to church on Sundays. He does not see the need to fellowship with God's people. He may even challenge the authority of Scriptures because, in his own eyes, he is now more enlightened. The situation looks bleak. Your worst nightmare is confirmed. Your "child" is no longer walking in the precepts of God.

I want to encourage you to stand. Yes, stand. Do not lean on your oars. Do not throw in the towel. Do not give up. The Bible states, *"having done all to stand."* This is God's admonition to you. Stand and believe that your child will rise to conquer. Stand in your conviction that your child will be saved. Having done all you could for him in his childhood, now stand that your child will conquer.

> *"Wherefore take unto you the whole armor of God, that ye may be able to withstand in the evil day, and having done all, to stand. Stand therefore, having your loins girt about with truth, and having on the breastplate of righteousness."*
>
> *Ephesians (6:13,14)*

After you have done all, remember that God has given you authority. In the evil day when the enemy is fighting against you through your seed, stand firm to fight back. Claim the promise of God for your children, no matter their age. It is your right that your seed will conquer with you.

Never allow yourself to be convinced by the devil that you have lost the battle in the life of your seed. Paul says to put on the whole armor of God. Why do you need the whole armor of God? Because, the armor is designed to do your battles for you. It is the armor, not of man, but of God. It has the authority of God in it and it is effective.

The battle you are involved in is not against flesh and blood, but against the forces of darkness that are at work in the heart of your child. Paul pointed out that the spirit of blindness is blindfolding the eyes of people from receiving the salvation of God. With the armor of God, you can let them lose, the only weapon that can work against these forces.

> *"Finally, my brethren, be strong in the Lord, and in the power of his might. Put on the whole armour of God, that ye may be able to stand against the wiles of the devil. For we wrestle not against flesh and blood, but against principalities, against powers,*

against the rulers of the darkness of this world, against spiritual wickedness in high places. Wherefore take unto you the whole armour of God, that ye may be able to withstand in the evil day, and having done all, to stand. Stand therefore, having your loins girt about with truth, and having on the breastplate of righteousness; And your feet shod with the preparation of the gospel of peace; Above all, taking the shield of faith, wherewith ye shall be able to quench all the fiery darts of the wicked. And take the helmet of salvation, and the sword of the Spirit, which is the word of God: Praying always with all prayer and supplication in the Spirit, and watching thereunto with all perseverance and supplication for all saints."

(Ephesians 6:10-18)

The armor of God is available. But, you must put it on. Yes, consciously and deliberately put it on. It will fight the enemy for you. So long as you put on each piece, without leaving any part unprotected, you can stand firm.

Truth

..having your loins girt about with truth ...

Paul lists the pieces of the armor, each playing a significant role. The first on the list is the truth. Stand firm in the truth that what God said in his Word He is able to perform. His Word will never pass away. It is the truth that will set you and your seed from the bondage of satan. God's Word says that you and

Search the Scriptures for the promises of God in regard to your children.

your family will be saved. A free citizen fights with force because he will not let the enemy take his land. You must fight to take your child for Christ. It is the truth of God's Word.

Jesus says that you will know the truth and the truth will set you free. The truth of God is your girdle around your loins. A girdle binds some of the pieces of the armour in place. A girdle gives the impression that you are ready for battle. As a free citizen, you must fight. God has promised you that He is willing to save your child. Let that truth always stand in your mind. Hold on to it as you will hold on to life. Do not allow the devil to dissuade you from it. Do not even entertain the thought that he will not come back to the Lord. With the truth of God as your girdle, you must fight on. Let the truth of God's Word set you free from any despair about your child's condition.

Righteousness

> *... and having on the breastplate of righteousness...*

The breastplate of righteousness comes next. Christ is your righteousness. Your child has a chance of being sanctified because of

Just as a breastplate guards the heart, so let the righteousness of Christ guard your heart.

your relationship with Christ. This is Paul's teaching in his epistle to Corinth. In addressing the problems of a believer who has an unbelieving spouse, Paul made a passing remark about the children in the home. He wrote:

> *For the unbelieving husband is sanctified by the wife, and the unbelieving wife is santified by the husband: else were your children unclean; but now are they holy.*
> *1 Corinthians 7:14*

The Gospel

> *... And your feet shod with the preparation of the gospel of peace...*

I have observed many mothers whose seeds have strayed from God. These mothers are guilt-ridden. Some of them are afraid to even broach on the topic of Christ. I remember one particular mother who said she had not as much mentioned the Gospel to her son for fear that he might run away. What a wrong notion! How could you remove medicine from a sick child because he might not like the taste! The Gospel is invested with the power of God to save lives.

Peter was not afraid that the Jews might reject Christ, who had been publicly crucified before them. He could have said, "Oh well, we have told them several times before that Jesus of Nazareth was the promised Messiah. Why should I continue to share it with them again? They have heard it before" But such attitude was foreign to Peter.

The Gospel is invested with the power of God to save lives.

On the day of Pentecost, he arose and gave the same Gospel to the same Jews that had heard of the Gospel before. The result? Three thousand were added to the Church. Some time later, after the miraculous healing of the lame man, the same Gospel was preached, and five thousand were brought to the saving knowledge of Christ.

There is still power in the Gospel of Christ. Have you presented your child with the Gospel of Christ before? Perhaps you yourself just gave your life to Christ, and so your child was not adequately exposed to the Lord. Then present the Gospel of Christ to him. And if you have given the Gospel to him before, give it to him again.

I told her that she was on the wrong track because she was withholding one of the weapons of God with which she could fight the enemy in her son's life. I advised her to remind her son regularly that Jesus loves him.

It was not up to a month that the same mother returned with the wayward son to our regularly scheduled meetings. God used the power of the Gospel to change that son for the better. His life was changed to the glory of God.

Faith

> *...Above all, taking the shield of faith, wherewith ye shall be able to quench all the fiery darts of the wicked...*

Another weapon of warfare is the shield of faith. The devil will tell you that there is no hope because your seed is gone for good. Remember that to the one who lives by faith all things are possible. Hope is still in the horizon. Stand firm by faith for your seed and claim the promise of God. Remember, he shall possess the gates of the enemy because of you. Lift up your shield in confidence and eliminate his darts of doubt, fear and despair. Believe God that He will touch the heart of your child. Hold on to God for mercy on your child.

Your faith will defeat every suggestion the enemy might bring.

When you believe God, God is pleased. Hebrews 11, verse 6 tells us that without the element of faith, we cannot please God. By the same token, with faith, you can please God. God will work mightily on behalf of the one whose heart trusts in the Lord.

Hebrews chapter 11 gives us a catalogue of men and women who pleased God through their faith. The faith of Abel won him God's approval of his sacrifice. Enoch was exempted from death because of his faith in God. Noah's faith saved him and his family from the flood. Abraham, through faith, fathered a son in his old age, when all hope had been lost. But his faith paid off. The son of promise was born.

Constantly confess the word of the Lord about your offspring.

Sarah, at ninety, became a mother for the first time, because she judged God that He would hold on to his promise.

Moses, through faith, became the law-giver, and the one who led Israel out of the land of bondage with great and unprecedented miracles. Daniel, through his faith, stayed in the midst of lions, unharmed. Faith placed in the Almighty God has made the impossible possible.

The same faith will bring your child back. Let your faith in God be constant. Jesus says you are to have faith in God. With unswerving faith, the devil's fiery darts will not harm you. Your faith will defeat every suggestion the enemy might bring. As soon as the devil comes with a negative thought, you can reply him, "It is written, ..." You then quote whatever passage that is germane to your situation. The devil must leave. Why? Because you have submitted to God and you are resisting him with the Word of God, and he has no option but to leave you. Let this truth be embedded in you.

"Submit yourselves therefore to God. Resist the devil, and he will flee from you."

James 4:7

Salvation

...And take the helmet of salvation...

The helmet of salvation is the other weapon we are admonished to utilize. Your

Your salvation has to do with your position - a reminder and assertion to satan that you belong to a different Kingdom.

salvation has to do with your position - a reminder and assertion to satan that you belong to a different Kingdom. Your head is crowned with God's love and grace. Put it on at all times. Put it on at all times and lean on the Lord to see you through in your fight against the devil.

The Word of God

> *... and the sword of the Spirit, which is the word of God...*

I have been talking about a defensive battle on behalf of your seed. But the apostle challenges us to now move forward offensively. Take the Sword of the Spirit which is the Word of God. Attack the enemy with the word of God. Tear down his barriers, his plans and purposes for your seed. The Word of God is the Sword of the Spirit. It is sharper than any two edged sword. It will pierce through the heart of your child. It will attack

As soon as the devil comes with a negative thought, you can reply him, "It is written, ..."

the spirit of the enemy in his life. Constantly confess the word of the Lord about your offspring. Confess the Word of God which says that great shall be the peace of your children. Confess that your children shall serve the Lord. Confess the written Word of God that no evil shall come near their dwelling place. Confess the Word of God that your children shall love the Lord God with all their heart.

Search the Scriptures for the promises of God in regard to your children. What do you do with the Scriptures? Confess and believe them. You can also use them to plead your cause before the Lord. And that brings us to the next weapon.

Prayer

> *...Praying always with all prayer and supplication in the Spirit...*

The other offensive weapon of this warfare is the prayer. Never cease to pray continuously for your seed. Even though he or she is behind prison wall, send your prayer.

A drug addicted son cried out to the mother in one of our counseling sessions, "Why don't you give me a break; night and

> ***Prayer wins the battle over the soul of your child in the spiritual realm***

day, I am tormented by your prayers." Prayer does work. It is a powerful weapon that God has given to you. Use it. Remember there is no distance with prayer. Prayer wins the battle over the soul of your child in the spiritual realm. It attacks the forces of darkness that are distracting him. It sets free his will to serve God.

You too can see the travail of your soul over your child

Prayer enables him to see for himself the repercussion of living a life without God. It makes him uncomfortable about the life he is leading. It accentuates the hunger within which only God can fill. Prayer is a great ammunition. It is the power God has placed within your power. Oh, how many mothers and fathers have prayed for their wayward children! Many saw the travail of their soul, and they were satisfied.

You too can see the travail of your soul over your child. Prayer is a travail. It can be laborious, but it must be done. His eternity is at stake. Your prayer is a great force to win him back to the kingdom of God. Thank God for prayer. There is no level that prayer cannot penetrate. Pray and watch for your victory through your seed.

The Sum of It

Your children are your heritage. They are God's gift for you to cherish. But with the responsibility comes the accountability. You are called to raise them up in a godly way. God is your strength. He is willing and able to give you the strength and the energy to bring them up.

When you bring them up in the way that they should go, joy and pride await you. On the contrary, if they do not receive the diligent teaching of God's Word in a loving atmosphere, they may become a problem in the future. It is in their early age that you must claim them for the Lord. Their souls must be claimed for the Lord our God. They can walk with God just like you. They can, like Noah's children, love the Kingdom of God and promote it.

Heaven must be our eternal destiny in Jesus' precious Name. Amen. God bless you as you sow the seed of eternal life in your children.

Other Books By The Same Author

Doubt Reduces God To Your Size

Doubt Reduces God To Your Size explores not only the various levels of faith but powerfully brings out how faith is the ingredient that unleashes the abundances of God's blessings on the child of God. The *principles* and the *how to* of believing God makes this book a must for every Christian who wants to believe God for all his needs - be it spiritual, physical or emotional. This book will teach you how to believe God and avoid doubt.

Ambassadorial Principles

We are ambassadors in this world. But to be effective in our calling, we must have principles that will ensure success. This book draws insights from the Word of God and demonstrates that God has indeed laid for us how to be the ambassadors He has called us to be. It is a book that will change everyone who wants to be God's representative here on earth.

Conquer With Your Seed

Conquer With Your Seed frankly calls parents to involve their children in their spiritual journey to the promised land. This book brings hope from the Word of God that inspite of the spiritual decline and depravity of today's society, Christian parents may still count on God to supply them with wisdom and wherewithal to raise up godly children. It is the book that will spark new revelation and hope for your children.

About The Book

Conquer With Your Seed frankly calls parents to involve their children in their spiritual journey to the promised land. This book brings hope from the Word of God that in spite of the spiritual decline and depravity of today's society, Christian parents may still count on God to supply them with wisdom and wherewithal to raise up godly children. It is the book that will spark new revelation and hope for raising up your child.

New Covenant Publications
Bronx, New York